NOBODY'S PERFECT, CHARLIE BROWN

CHARLES M. SCHULZ

Selected Cartoons from
YOU CAN DO IT, CHARLIE BROWN Vol. I

A FAWCETT CREST BOOK
Fawcett Publications, Inc., Greenwich, Conn.

NOBODY'S PERFECT, CHARLIE BROWN

This book, prepared especially for Fawcett Publications, Inc., com-
prises the first half of YOU CAN DO IT, CHARLIE BROWN, and
is reprinted by arrangement with Holt, Rinehart and Winston, Inc.

Published by Fawcett World Library
67 West 44th Street, New York, N. Y. 10036
Printed in the United States of America

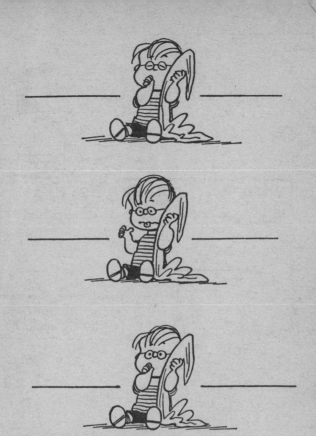

SOME DAYS I TASTE LIKE AN INFERIOR BRAND!

I WONDER IF THE STARS REALLY DO HAVE LITTLE POINTS...

NO, THIS IS DUE TO OUR ASTIGMATISM, WHICH IS A DISTORTION OF VISION CAUSED BY IRREGULARITIES IN THE SURFACE OF THE CORNEA

MY OPHTHALMOLOGIST SAYS THAT A SLIGHT DEGREE OF ASTIGMATISM IS NORMAL, AND THIS KEEPS US FROM SEEING THE STARS AS ROUND DOTS OF LIGHT

TELL YOUR OPHTHALMOLOGIST HE'S RUINED MY STAR-GAZING!

WHY COULDN'T McCOVEY HAVE HIT THE BALL JUST THREE FEET HIGHER?

WHEN I LOOK FORWARD TO A BALL GAME, I DON'T WANT TO BE DISAPPOINTED

I DON'T SEE WHY A LITTLE RAIN SHOULD KEEP EVERYBODY AWAY! IF I CAN SHOW UP TO PLAY, I DON'T SEE WHY THE OTHERS CAN'T!

MAYBE I'M JUST MORE DETERMINED THAN THEY ARE.. MAYBE I'M JUST MORE STUBBORN..

..MAYBE I'M JUST MORE STUPID!

HERE'S A LETTER FROM BODEGA BAY, CALIFORNIA...

"DEAR LINUS, OUR FAMILY WAS ON A PICNIC YESTERDAY, AND WE THINK WE SAW YOUR BLANKET... WE CHASED IT ACROSS A FIELD, BUT COULDN'T CATCH IT..."

"THE LAST WE SAW OF IT, IT WAS FLYING HIGHER AND HIGHER, AND WAS HEADED OUT OVER THE...

......GOOD GRIEF... OCEAN!"

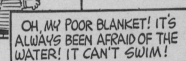

OR WHY COULDN'T McCOVEY HAVE HIT THE BALL EVEN **TWO** FEET HIGHER?

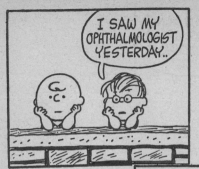

I SAW MY OPHTHALMOLOGIST YESTERDAY..

HE SAID I MAY NOT HAVE TO WEAR MY GLASSES ALL THE TIME..HE ALSO SAID HE SHOT AN EIGHTY A FEW DAYS AGO...

YOU TALKED ABOUT GOLF?

OH, YES... I ALWAYS ASK HIM ABOUT HIS GOLF GAME...

IT PUTS HIM AT EASE DURING THE EXAMINATION

I'M SORRY, CHARLIE BROWN, BUT I GUESS I'LL QUIT, TOO..

IT'S HARD TO PLAY ON A TEAM THAT ALWAYS LOSES... IT'S DEPRESSING... I'M THE KIND WHO NEEDS TO WIN NOW AND THEN..WITH YOU, IT'S DIFFERENT..

I THINK YOU GET SORT OF A NEUROTIC PLEASURE OUT OF LOSING ALL THE TIME...

"LITTLE LEAGUE" PSYCHIATRY!

MY WHOLE TEAM HAS DESERTED ME!

ALL I'M LEFT WITH IS BAD MEMORIES AND A PILE OF EMPTY BASEBALL CAPS...

EVEN CASEY STENGEL COULDN'T DO **THAT!**

I GUESS LINUS IS PRETTY USED TO HIS GLASSES BY THIS TIME..

OH, YES... INCIDENTALLY, I THINK HE'S MYOPIC...

REALLY?

ASK HIM WHO'S GOING TO WIN THE NATIONAL LEAGUE PENNANT

WELL, SALLY, TODAY'S THE FIRST DAY OF SCHOOL...

WE'LL SOON BE THERE...JUST A LITTLE WAY TO GO NOW...

THERE IT IS...THERE'S YOUR SCHOOL...

AAUGH!

STOP GRINNING AT ME!

DO YOU PARTICIPATE MUCH IN KINDERGARTEN, SALLY?

I TRY NOT TO...I'M SORT OF HOLDING BACK...

FOR INSTANCE, YESTERDAY THE TEACHER WANTED ALL OF US TO GO TO THE CHALK BOARD AND DRAW, BUT I GOT OUT OF IT...

I TOLD HER IT WAS HARD FOR ME BECAUSE OF MY BURSITIS!

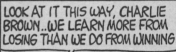

DEAR GREAT PUMPKIN,
I AM LOOKING FORWARD
TO YOUR ARRIVAL ON
HALLOWEEN NIGHT.

I HOPE YOU WILL BRING
ME LOTS OF PRESENTS.

EVERYONE TELLS ME YOU ARE
A FAKE, BUT I BELIEVE IN
YOU.
      SINCERELY,
  LINUS VAN PELT

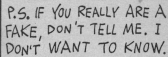

P.S. IF YOU REALLY ARE A
FAKE, DON'T TELL ME. I
DON'T WANT TO KNOW.

THIS IS THE TIME OF YEAR TO WRITE TO THE "GREAT PUMPKIN"

ON HALLOWEEN NIGHT HE RISES OUT OF THE PUMPKIN PATCH, AND FLIES THROUGH THE AIR WITH HIS BAG OF TOYS FOR ALL THE CHILDREN!

I'M WRITING TO HIM NOW...DO YOU WANT ME TO PUT IN A GOOD WORD FOR YOU, CHARLIE BROWN?

BY ALL MEANS...I CAN USE ALL THE INFLUENCE I CAN GET IN HIGH PLACES!

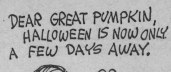

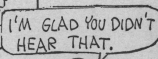

AND ON HALLOWEEN NIGHT THE "GREAT PUMPKIN" RISES OUT OF THE PUMPKIN PATCH...

THEN HE FLIES THROUGH THE AIR TO BRING TOYS TO ALL THE GOOD LITTLE CHILDREN EVERYWHERE!

THAT'S A GOOD STORY...

I PLACE IT JUST A LITTLE BELOW THE ONE ABOUT THE FLYING REINDEER!

STRIKE THREE!

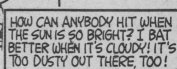

THIS BAT IS NO GOOD! IT'S TOO LIGHT! THAT BALL THEY'RE USING IS NO GOOD EITHER!

HOW CAN ANYBODY HIT WHEN THE SUN IS SO BRIGHT? I BAT BETTER WHEN IT'S CLOUDY! IT'S TOO DUSTY OUT THERE, TOO!

I CAN'T HIT WELL WHEN THE WIND IS BLOWING! THAT BAT I WAS USING IS TOO SHORT! IT'S HARD TO SEE THE BALL TODAY! YOU CAN'T HIT A BALL WHEN THE BAT IS TOO THIN! I THINK THEIR PITCHER IS..

GOOD GRIEF!

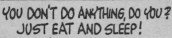

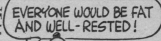

DEAR PENCIL-PAL,
I AM SORRY I
HAVEN'T WRITTEN.

IT SEEMS AS IF I AM
ALWAYS APOLOGIZING,
DOESN'T IT?

WELL, I AM SORRY THAT
I HAVEN'T WRITTEN BEFORE.
I GUESS I AM A POOR
CORRESPONDENT.

PLEASE FORGIVE ME FOR
NOT WRITING SOONER.
HOW HAVE YOU BEEN?
YOURS TRULY,
CHARLIE BROWN